MATH MASTERS: ANALYZE THIS!

PRISMS and PYRAMIDS

Melanie Alvarez

Rourke
Educational Media

rourkeeducationalmedia.com

Before Reading:

Building Academic Vocabulary and Background Knowledge

Before reading a book, it is important to tap into what your child or students already know about the topic. This will help them develop their vocabulary, increase their reading comprehension, and make connections across the curriculum.

1. *Look at the cover of the book. What will this book be about?*
2. *What do you already know about the topic?*
3. *Let's study the Table of Contents. What will you learn about in the book's chapters?*
4. *What would you like to learn about this topic? Do you think you might learn about it from this book? Why or why not?*
5. *Use a reading journal to write about your knowledge of this topic. Record what you already know about the topic and what you hope to learn about the topic.*
6. *Read the book.*
7. *In your reading journal, record what you learned about the topic and your response to the book.*
8. *After reading the book complete the activities below.*

Content Area Vocabulary
Read the list. What do these words mean?

classified
congruent
consist
construct
determining
diagonally
irregular
measurable
sum

After Reading:

Comprehension and Extension Activity

After reading the book, work on the following questions with your child or students in order to check their level of reading comprehension and content mastery.

1. *How many measurable dimensions do two-dimensional shapes have?* (Summarize)
2. *What is the difference between a regular and irregular polygon?* (Infer)
3. *What does the base of a figure tell you?* (Asking questions)
4. *How are three-dimensional shapes classified?* (Text to self connection)
5. *How do you calculate the surface area of an object?* (Asking questions)

Extension Activity

Practice all the concepts in the book to master prisms and pyramids!

Table of Contents

The Second Dimension—2-D Shapes

Before we get to 3-D figures like prisms or pyramids, we need to learn about two-dimensional shapes. Two-dimensional (2-D) shapes have two **measureable** dimensions: length and width, but no thickness. Each 2-D shape is located on a flat plane. If you are thinking about airplanes, then you have the wrong planes! A plane is a flat surface that extends forever in all directions. It has no thickness.

You can think of it as a flat floor! Many video games use planes as the surface for your favorite video game characters to roam around on!

Some examples of two-dimensional shapes include triangles, squares, and circles.

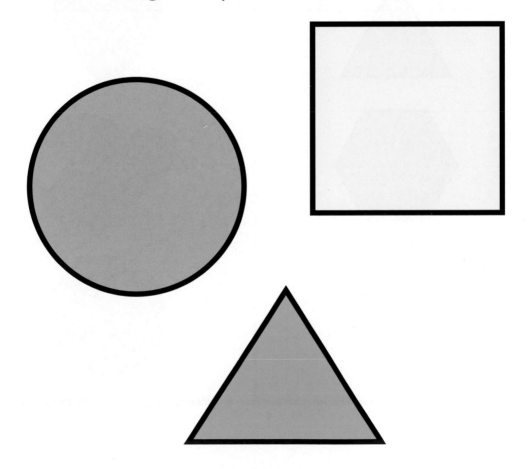

Polygons are closed, two-dimensional figures that **consist** of only straight lines.

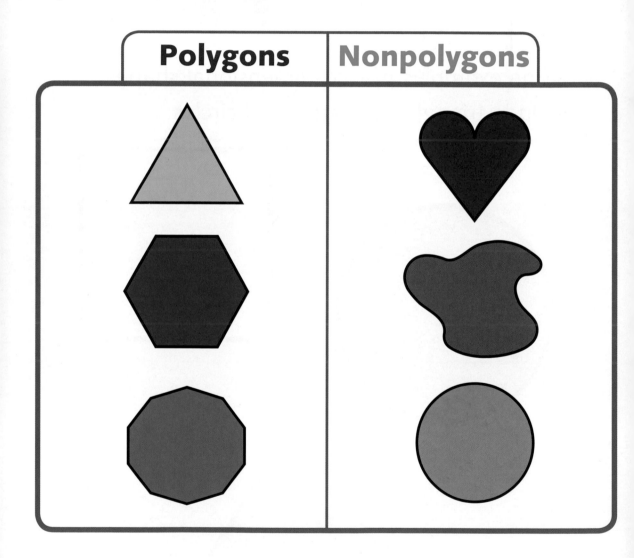

| **Polygons** | **Nonpolygons** |

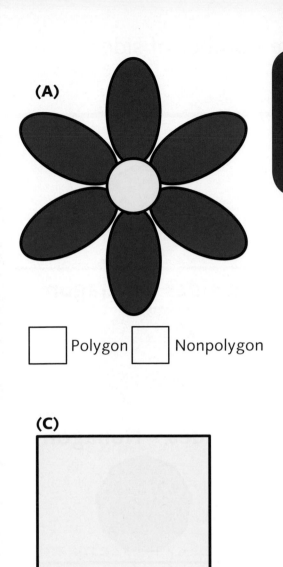

(A)

☐ Polygon ☐ Nonpolygon

Remember to be a polygon the shape needs to be:
- closed
- flat
- have no curves

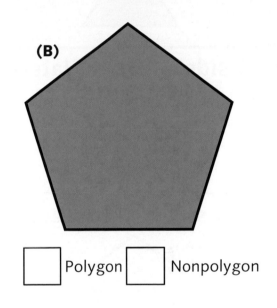

(B)

☐ Polygon ☐ Nonpolygon

(C)

☐ Polygon ☐ Nonpolygon

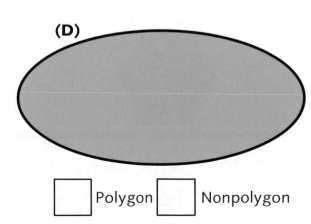

(D)

☐ Polygon ☐ Nonpolygon

Answers:

A: Nonpolygon; B: Polygon;
C: Polygon; D: Nonpolygon

Polygons are named by the number of sides they have.

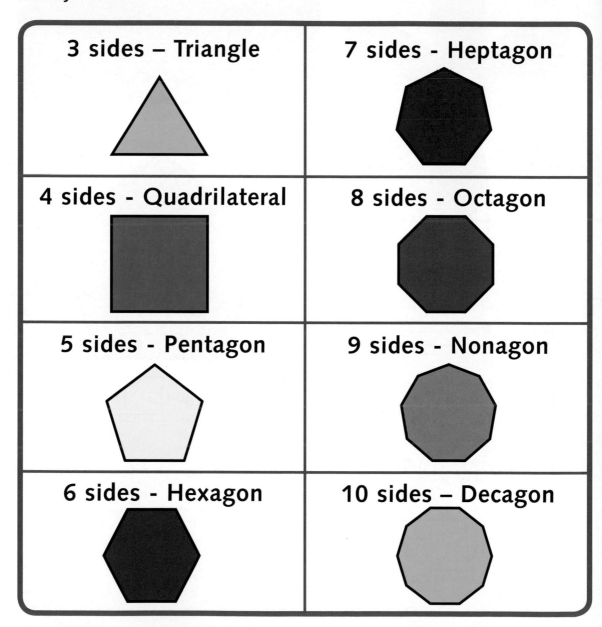

3 sides – Triangle	7 sides - Heptagon
4 sides - Quadrilateral	8 sides - Octagon
5 sides - Pentagon	9 sides - Nonagon
6 sides - Hexagon	10 sides – Decagon

Polygons with many sides are named using numbers. For example, a polygon with 52 sides is a 52-gon.

Some polygons are regular and some are **irregular**. Polygons can be considered regular if their sides have the same length and their angles have the same measure.

Regular or Irregular? Name that Polygon!

(A)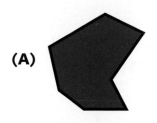

(B)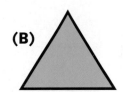

(C)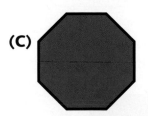

(D)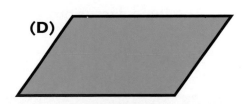

(E)

(F)

Journey to the Third Dimension

Three-dimensional (3-D) shapes have three dimensions: length, width, and height.

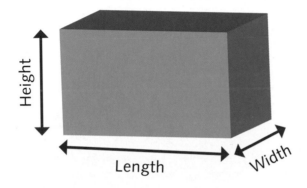

The three dimensions give figures their volume.

3-D movies are exciting to watch because they include the third dimension: depth. Depth is the distance from the front to the back of a figure. Objects in the movie seem to pop off the screen at you!

Examples of three-dimensional figures include cubes, pyramids, prisms, and cylinders.

Prisms and pyramids are examples of three-dimensional figures that have polygon-shaped flat sides called faces. Faces are flat surfaces that meet at the edge of a shape.

All About the Base

Bases are specific types of faces. The base of a figure is the face (or faces) that is perpendicular to the height.

Lines or planes are perpendicular to each other when they meet or cross at right (90°) angles. This forms a T or plus-sign shape.

The main difference between pyramids and prisms are the number of bases.

Pyramids have one base, which is the face of the figure that is considered the bottom.

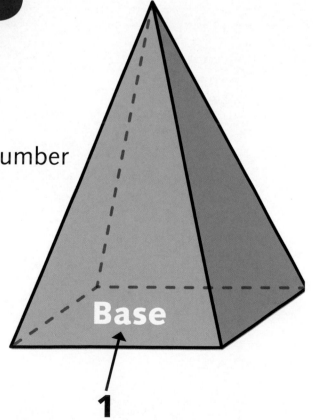

Base

1

When people think of pyramids, usually the pyramids of Egypt come to mind; however, pyramids can have a variety of polygon-shaped bases.

Prisms have two bases, which are the faces of the figure that are considered the top and bottom. These bases are parallel to each other and are **congruent** shapes.

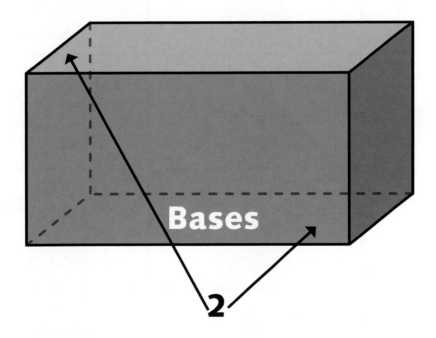

Prisms are like pyramids in that they, too, can have many types of polygons for bases.

Both pyramids and prisms are named after their bases.

Base	Pyramid Name	Prism Name
Triangle	Triangular Pyramid	Triangular Prism
Square	Square Pyramid	Square Prism (or Cube)
Rectangle	Rectangular Pyramid	Rectangular Prism
Pentagon	Pentagonal Pyramid	Pentagonal Prism
Hexagon	Hexagonal Pyramid	Hexagonal Prism

Another reason bases are important in understanding prisms and pyramids is that you use the area of the base to calculate volume and surface area.

To calculate the area of the base, use the area formula for whichever polygon the base is. If the base, for example, is a rectangle, then multiply the length times the width to get the area of the base.

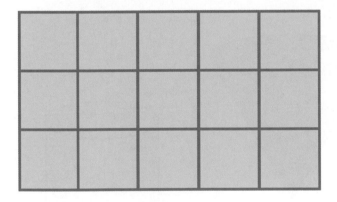

3 × 5 = 15

Area = 15 square units

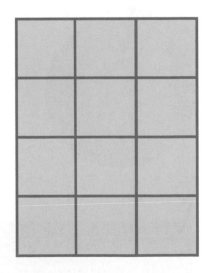

4 × 3 = 12

Area = 12 square units

Faces, Vertices, and Edges

Three-dimensional shapes are **classified** by the number and size of their faces and edges, and by their number of vertices.

Prisms and pyramids are classified as polyhedra because they are made of flat faces. Examples of non-polyhedra shapes would be spheres, cylinders, and cones.

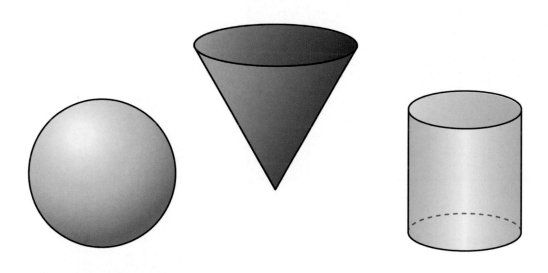

The word "polyhedra" comes from the Greek the Greek words *poly*, meaning *many*, and *hedra*, meaning *faces*.

We have already explored faces. So, what are edges and vertices?

An edge is where two faces of a three-dimensional figure meet.

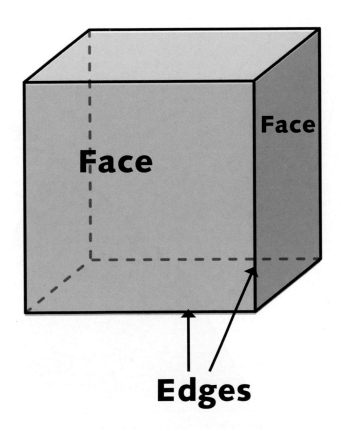

Face

Face

Edges

A vertex (or if there are more than one: vertices) is where three or more faces meet to form what we think of as a corner. One of the vertices of pyramids has a specific name: the apex. The apex is the vertex that is opposite the base of a pyramid: the point that makes a pyramid a pyramid.

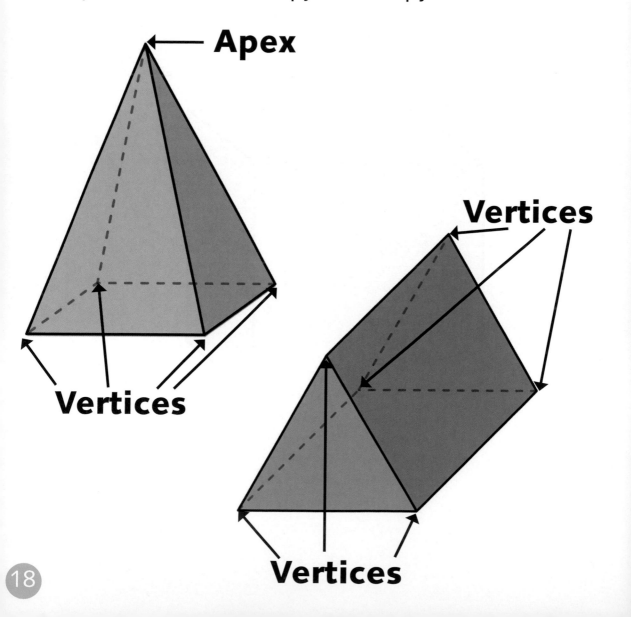

Apex

Vertices

Vertices

Vertices

3-D Figures	#of Faces	#of Edges	#of Vertices
Cube (square prism)	6	12	8
Rectangular Prism	6	12	8
Hexagonal Prism	8	18	12
Triangular Prism	5	9	6
Square Pyramid	5	8	5
Triangular Pyramid	4	6	4

Exploring Volume

Volume is the measure of space that a three-dimensional object takes up. It is measured in cubic units, like cm³.

To find the volume of a prism, you multiply the area of its base times the height.

Some prisms are easier to calculate the volume of than others. Let's focus on finding the volume of rectangular prisms and triangular prisms.

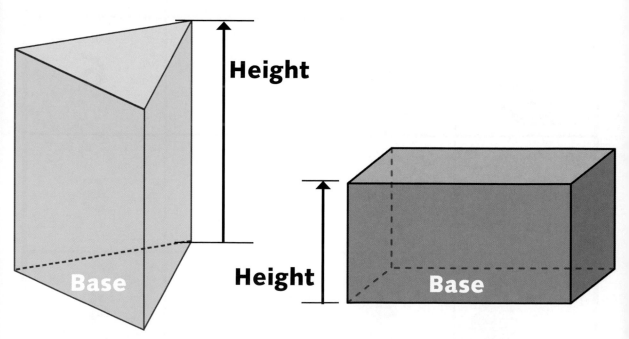

Volume = Area of the Base x Height

The formula for finding the volume of a rectangular prism is: V= B h, where B equals the area of the base. This formula works for the volume of a cube as well, because a cube is a square prism, and a square is a type of rectangle.

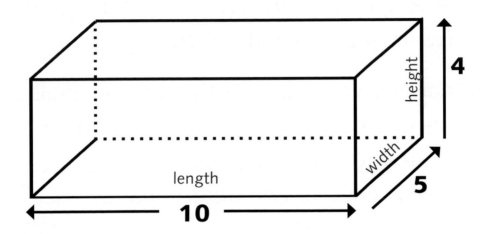

The volume of this rectangular prism would be 200 cubic units, because 10 units x 5 units x 4 units is 200 cubic units.

You try!

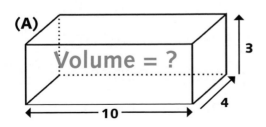

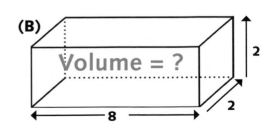

Answers:

21

The formula for finding the volume of a triangular prism is essentially the same: V= B x h, where B equals the area of the base. The difference, however, is that calculating the area of the base is different for triangles than it is for rectangles. With rectangles you can use a simple length (l) width (w) formula to find the area.

With triangles you must cut that area formula in half. This is because a rectangle is made up of two triangles. If you cut a rectangle in half **diagonally**, you get two right triangles.

So, the formula for the volume of a triangular prism can also be written as:

$$\frac{V= \text{length x width x height}}{2}$$

Example: Anabella built a model of a triangular prism. The bases were triangles with areas of 6 in². The height of the model was 8 inches. What was the volume of her triangular prism?

6 in² x 8 in = 48 in³, so the volume of the triangular prism is 48 in³

As you may guess, calculating the volume of pyramids is quite different than calculating the volume of prisms.

Since pyramids come to an apex point, you calculate the volume by multiplying $\frac{1}{3}$ times the area of the base times the height of the prism. This works for all pyramids. $V = \frac{1}{3}Bh$

B = area of the base of the pyramid
h = height of the pyramid

Example: Gracie bought a model of a square pyramid at the museum store. The square base had an area of 121cm² and the height of the pyramid was 6cm.

What was the volume of the square pyramid?

121cm² x 6cm = 726 cm³ so the volume of the square pyramid is 726 units³

Exploring Surface Area

If you know how to calculate the area of polygons like rectangles and triangles, then you know how to find the surface area of some prisms!

Surface area is the area of each face of a three-dimensional object added up. It is measured in squared units. One way of **determining** surface area is to draw or **construct** a net. A net is the two-dimensional pattern of a three-dimensional shape. If you fold a figure's net, you will create the 3-D figure.

Here is one net of a rectangular prism.

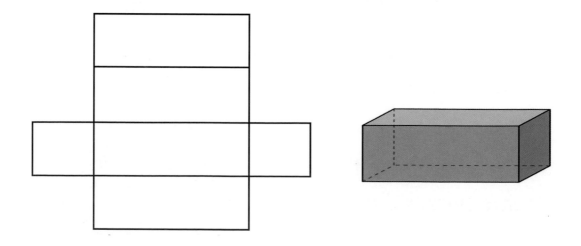

If you find the **sum** of the area of each of the prism's rectangular faces, and add those to the area of both bases, you will get the total surface area of the rectangular prism! Think of surface area almost as wrapping paper, but with no overlapping paper.

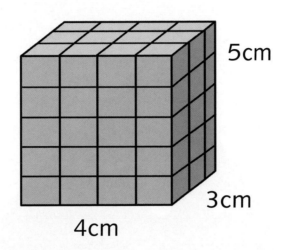

5cm

3cm

4cm

What would the surface area of this prism be?

SA = 2 (Area of the top) + 2 (Area of the front) + 2 (Area of the side)

SA = 2 (3cm x 4cm) + 2 (4cm x 5cm) + 2 (3cm x 5cm)

SA = 24 cm² + 40 cm² + 30 cm²

SA = 94 cm²

Finding the surface area of pyramids is essentially the same: you add up the area of each face, including the base. Remember, you will need to know how to find the area of a triangle, since pyramids have triangular faces.

Nets (Not the Fishing or Basketball Kind)

Let's go back and look at nets again. Notice that in any type of prism the faces (not including the bases) are all rectangles. However, in any type of pyramid, the faces (not including the bases) are all triangles. This is because pyramids come to a point (the apex).

Let's look at nets of prisms and pyramids.

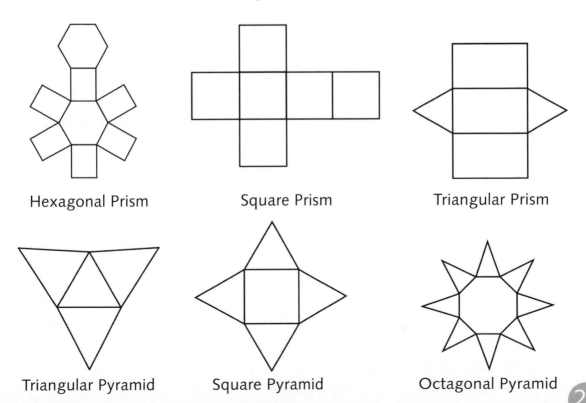

Hexagonal Prism   Square Prism   Triangular Prism

Triangular Pyramid   Square Pyramid   Octagonal Pyramid

Now let's picture folding each net up around its base (or bases). Can you see how this would construct the 3-D shape?

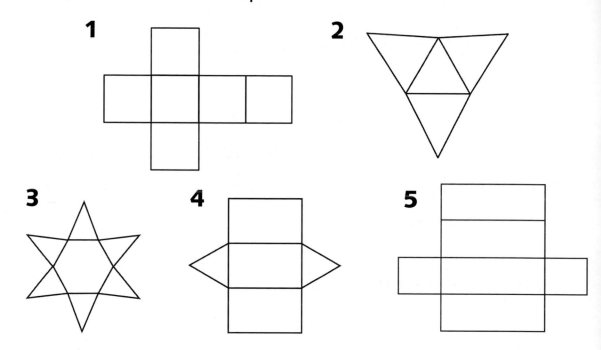

When you are trying to determine the name of a figure based on its net, think of these handy steps:

1. **Number of faces:** If it is one base with faces coming off of it, then it is a pyramid. If you find two congruent bases, then it is a prism.

2. **Shape of the faces:** If there are only triangular faces attached to the base, then it is a pyramid. If there are rectangular faces, then it is a prism.

3. **Shape of the base:** In order to determine what type of pyramid or prism it is, look at the base or bases. The shape of the base names the 3-D figure.

Find the nets of the following three-dimensional figures: **(A)** hexagonal pyramid; **(B)** rectangular prism; **(C)** cube or square prism; **(D)** triangular prism; **(E)** triangular pyramid

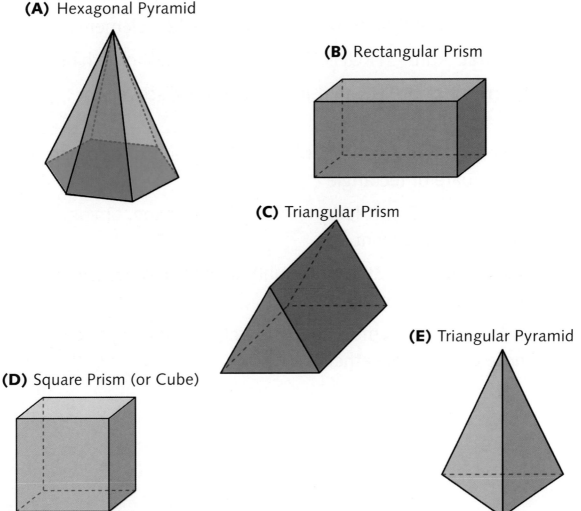

(A) Hexagonal Pyramid

(B) Rectangular Prism

(C) Triangular Prism

(E) Triangular Pyramid

(D) Square Prism (or Cube)

Which is your favorite net?

Glossary

classified (KLAS-uh-fide): to put things into groups according to the characteristics they have in common

congruent (kuhn-GROO-uhnt): equal in shape and size

consist (kuhn-SIST): to be made up of certain elements

construct (kuhn-STRUHKT): to make or build something

determining (di-TUR-min-ing): making a discovery or finding out

diagonally (dye-AG-uh-nuhl-ee): joining opposite corners of a square or rectangle

irregular (i-REG-yuh-lur): not standard in shape, timing, size, or arrangement

measureable (MEZH-ur-uh-buhl): able to find the size or weight of something

sum (suhm): the number that you get from adding two or more numbers together

Index

Websites to Visit

www.studyzone.org/testprep/math4/d/shapes4p.cfm

www.math-salamanders.com/3d-geometric-shapes.html

www.mathsisfun.com/geometry/pyramids.html

About The Author

Melanie M. Alvarez is a sixth grade mathematics teacher at an environmentally focused charter school in Florida. When she is not working as a teacher, private tutor, or writer, she enjoys spending time with her husband and two sons. Melanie is a firm believer in the power of reading and in raising her children and students to be lifelong learners.

Meet The Author!
www.meetREMauthors.com

PHOTO CREDITS: Cover and title page © Tedgun, brain/lightbulb © Positive Vectors; page 4 © Mario © Tinxi, flags © olegganko, cookies © exopixel; pages 10 and 26 3D shapes © trexdruid, pages 11-20, 22-24 and 29 3d shapes © aekikuis, pyramid photo © Waj; page 20 triangular prism © V_ctoria   All images from Shutterstock.com

Edited by: Keli Sipperley

Cover and Interior design by: Nicola Stratford   www.nicolastratford.com

Library of Congress PCN Data

Prisms and Pyramids / Melanie M. Alvarez
 (Math Masters: Analyze This!)
 ISBN 978-1-68191-735-1 (hard cover)
 ISBN 978-1-68191-836-5 (soft cover)
 ISBN 978-1-68191-929-4 (e-Book)
Library of Congress Control Number: 2016932657

Rourke Educational Media
Printed in the United States of America, North Mankato, Minnesota

Also Available as: